Stories Untold
Jewish Pioneer Women
1850–1910

The Art
of
Andrea Kalinowski

A TRAVELING EXHIBITION
ORGANIZED BY THE MUSEUM OF FINE ARTS, SANTA FE
WITH GENEROUS SUPPORT FROM THE DOBKIN FAMILY FOUNDATION

CONTENTS

A JEWISH HOMESTEADER

To most immigrants, that is, Jewish immigrants, New York was America; some would dare venture as far as Chicago. They continued the trades they brought with them; they labored in sweatshops, peddled, or worked themselves up to the luxurious affluence of sweating it out seven days weekly in their own little candy or grocery stores. It was better than the Old Country, but not too different. They heard the same language, smelled the same musty odors in their synagogues. The rest of America was there, somewhere, but they knew and cared little about it.

But the Jewish immigrants who settled in the wilderness were different; they were a special breed. Each was a Moses in his own right, leading his people out of the land of bondage—out of czarist Russia, out of anti-Semitic Poland, out of Romania, and Galicia. Each was leading his family to a Promised Land: only this was no land flowing with milk and honey, no land of olive trees and vineyards.

This was a harsh, forbidding land. . . . The ground was there—good black soil beneath the prairie grass—but before it could be cultivated it had to be cleared. Before you could set plow to furrow you had to remove the rocks that strewed every foot of this land. . . .

What did it matter if the work was backbreaking, if the winters were severe and endless? The harsh winds of the prairie in winter were less bitter than the winds of oppression, hatred, and intolerance that had buffeted them in Europe.

. . . At the mercy of nature, their livelihood depended upon whether the rains came in time and the frosts not too soon. It depended on whether or not a prairie fire, fanned by the autumn winds and carried along by the tumbleweeds, which served as flaming torches, would consume the crops standing in stacks waiting for the thrashing machine. Fire might even destroy the house that you and your family had labored on.

Yes, it all could, and often did, happen. And yet it was nothing compared to the cruelty of man against man. It was still nature's caprice, not man's calculated cruelty. There would always be another spring, another rainfall, another sowing, and another harvesting.

Sophie Trupin

from *Dakota Diaspora: Memoirs of a Jewish Homesteader*

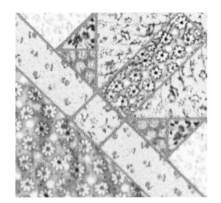

FANNY JAFFE SHARLIP *was born in Borosna, Russia, and arrived in the United States in 1889. She wrote her memoirs in 1947.*

My father seriously began to make plans to go to America. A good many things had to be settled. He decided to leave the family at home until he could establish himself. He was determined to go where Jews could worship God as they pleased, where they could breathe freedom, and where their lives were not threatened every minute of the day. . . .

Preparations were made for the great journey to America. Father wrote long instructions (to mother): First you apply for a government pass; every time you change trains, be sure to count the children; see that they are properly fed and get milk at every station; do not give the cow away until the last day, for the young ones need the milk.

The day came at last when we were to depart. My mother went to synagogue to say goodbye to our friends. I took out my prayer book and began to pray wholeheartedly, for the future looked uncertain and I felt the need of God's help. I noticed my sister Mary sewing hooks and eyes on her skirt. "On the Sabbath day!" I wailed. "You know what you're doing, you sinner you."

Mother came home from synagogue with a sad face, for it is hard to leave relatives and friends and the place where one is established. It was a tremendous undertaking: such a long journey with seven small children. . . .

We traveled steerage and it was not fit for dogs. I can still smell the terrible odor that made me so sick; my mother was very sensitive to smells so I came by it honestly. I was so ill that I didn't care whether I lived or died. Of course mother did some tall praying; she did not want to feed the fish with the bodies of her children. . . .

We had our share of storms on the high seas and the ship swayed unmercifully. There were good things to eat in the ship's store such as oranges, candy, cookies, and soda pop, but mother had no money to buy them for us. She went to the family who had befriended me and said, "Here is one of my rings. Please give me some money, I simply must buy some good things for my children to eat. You are also going to Philadelphia, here is my address. As soon as I am settled there I will redeem the ring."

The next morning we saw that great symbol of hope for the immigrant: The Statue of Liberty. Our hearts were filled with joy and thanksgiving. The authorities checked and examined us and I guess they were satisfied that we would make good citizens for they let us through.

All works are mixed media on canvas, and courtesy of the artist unless otherwise noted.

Fanny's Quilt 2001
98 × 100.5 inches
quilting assistance: Cindy Barfield, Amy Varner

Fanny Jaffe Sharlip immigrated to the United States in 1889 with her mother and six siblings. She wrote her memoirs in 1947. "Now my father began to make plans to go to America. A good many things had to be settled. He decided to leave the family home until he could establish himself. He was determined to go where Jews could worship God as they pleased, where they could breathe freedom, and where their life was not threatened every minute of the day—that was infinitely more important than money."

"Preparations were made for the great journey to America. Father wrote instructions (to mother): first apply for a government pass; every time you change trains, be sure to count the children; see that they are properly fed and get milk at every station; do not give the cow away until the last day for the young ones need the milk, etc., etc."

"The day came at last when we were to depart for America. It was Saturday, and my mother went to the Synagogue to say goodbye to our friends. I took out my prayer book and began to pray wholeheartedly for the future looked so uncertain and I felt the need of God's help. I noticed my sister Mary sewing hooks and eyes on her skirt. "On the Sabbath day!" I wailed, "You know what your doing, you sinner you."

"Mother came home from synagogue with a sad face, for it is hard to leave relatives and friends and the place where one is established and economically secure. It was a tremendous undertaking on such a long journey with seven small children. Uncle William came over to tie up bundles and pack the "carsinky" (a large suitcase made of fiber)."

"All of us were in the wagon and when the horses gave a pull and the wagon began to move, mother started to cry, but we refrained from tears in order to spare her additional trouble. We traveled about three days before we reached the Russian-German border. We had no difficulties crossing the Russian frontier, for we had all the necessary permits, but we were all relieved when we got off the train at Yatceon which was the first town in Germany after crossing the border."

"The German cars used to transport immigrants were unfit even for cattle. There were no benches, no toilets, no running water. The cars were locked so no one could get out until an important station was reached, which often meant a half a day or more. At last after four or five days we reached beautiful Berlin with its fine railroad station. From Berlin we traveled for about three days in the same horrible "cattle cars" to Hamburg which was the port from which we were to embark for the United States."

"We traveled steerage and it was not fit for dogs. I can still smell the terrible odor that made me so sick; my mother was very sensitive to smells so I came by it honestly. I was so ill that I didn't care whether I lived or died. Of course mother did some tall praying; she did not want to feed the fish with the bodies of her children. I practically lived on condensed milk which they fed to the babies, but the doctor ordered it for me even though I was too old for baby food, for it was about the only thing I could keep in my stomach."

"We had our share of storms on the high seas and the ship swayed unmercifully. There were good things to eat in the ship's store such as oranges, candy, cookies and soda pop, but mother had no money to by them for us. She went to the family who had befriended me and said, "Here is one of my rings. Please give me some money, I simply must buy some good things for my children to eat. You are going to Philadelphia also, here is my address, and as soon as I am settled there I will redeem the ring."

"The next morning we saw that great symbol of hope for the immigrant, the Statue of Liberty, and our hearts were filled with joy and thanksgiving. Castle Garden. The name does not fit the place-Stable Barn would be more proper. The authorities checked and examined us and I guess they were satisfied that we would make good citizens for they let us through."

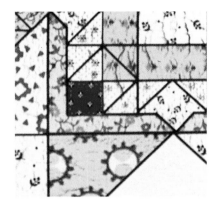

FANNY BROOKS *was born in 1837 in Schweidnitz, Germany, and arrived in the United States in 1853. She died in Wiesbaden, Germany, in 1901. Her story is narrated by her daughter, Eveline Auerbach.*

In 1852 Julius Brooks returned to his native village of Frankenstein having lived in America for five years. He met Fanny Bruck, who became intrigued by his tales of adventure and begged him to take her with him back to America. Fanny Bruck married Julius Brooks when she was sixteen. The newly-wed couple sailed at once from Hamburg to America. As was the custom in those days, the entire town of Frankenstein came to the train to see them off. They brought rice, flowers, old shoes, and called after them "Good Luck," "God-Speed," and "Early Return."

Fanny and Julius took a room at a boarding house on East 14th Street. In the spring of 1854, they left New York for Galena, Illinois, where they heard a company was leaving the following June for California. . . .

Ten individuals were allotted one wagon and tent. . . . They were supplied with 100 lbs. of flour, 50 lbs. of sugar, 50 lbs. of bacon, 50 lbs. of rice, 30 lbs. of beans, 20 lbs. of dried apples, 20 lbs. of dried peaches, 5 lbs. of tea, 1 gallon of vinegar, 10 bars of soap, and 25 lbs. of salt. These articles and the milk from their cows, the game caught on the plains and in the fresh water streams furnished them better food and more of it than they had had in their native land. Mother said the Yankees were lovely people but very wasteful and poor cooks. Their main forte was bread, pies, and hotcakes, ham or bacon and eggs. Their vegetables were cooked without taste and their meats either done to death or raw. . . .

Mother's first hardship was the lack of bread. After she ran out of hard tack and army bread, she found herself without any bread. As she had never baked bread before and was too bashful to ask any of the other women, she decided to try her luck. She put the flour and water in a pan, added some salt, and started to knead it as she had seen the other women do. She worked it an hour until she was tired, covered it over . . . left it to stand overnight to rise.

Next morning, bright and early she was up, put the dough in the skillet, and started her fire. She piled sagebrush, broomgrass, and buffalo chips below and above and watched it patiently for an hour. All at once she smelled something burning and found it was her bread. It was solid as a rock and black as coal. She was so disheartened she sat down and cried. Her neighbor asked what the trouble was. Mother told her. Her neighbor said: "Never mind, I have some nice biscuits and will give you enough for your breakfast, and tonight I will show you how to mix bread. No doubt you forgot the yeast." Mother had no idea that yeast was needed. That evening she was shown how to bake bread . . . and she taught them how to make German coffee cake.

Fanny Brooks's Quilt 2001
101 × 99.5 inches
quilting assistance: Cindy Barfield, Amy Varner

Fanny Brooks' story is narrated by her daughter, Eveline Auerbach. In 1852 Julius Brooks returned to his native village of Frankenstein having lived in America for five years. In that same year he met Fanny Bruck, who became intrigued by his tales of adventure and begged him to take her with him back to America. Fanny Bruck married Julius Brooks when she was 16 in August, of 1853. The newly wed couple sailed at once from Hamburg to America. As was the custom in those days, the entire town of Frankenstein came to the train to see them off. They brought rice, flowers, old shoes, and called after them "Good Luck", "God-Speed", and "Early Return".

Fanny and Julius took a room at a boarding house on East 14th Street.
In the spring of 1854, they left New York for Galena, Illinois where they heard that a company was leaving the following June for California. They had to go by boat from Galena to Florence, where they purchased a covered wagon and two little mules, in order to be comfortable; otherwise they would have been compelled to walk. Ten individuals were the number allotted to a wagon and one tent. One hundred pounds of luggage, including beds and clothing for all persons over eight years of age; fifty pounds to those between eight years and four years; all under four years of age had no luggage privileges.

The wagon bed was 12 feet long, 3 feet 4 inches wide, and 18 inches deep. Boxes were made to fit inside the wagons to put utensils and clothing in. Each wagon this year cost $65.00. They were supplied with 100 lbs. of flour, 50 lbs. of sugar, 50 lbs. of bacon, 50 lbs. of rice, 30 lbs. of beans, 20 lbs. dried peaches, 5 lbs. of tea, 1 gallon of vinegar, 10 bars of soap, 25 lbs. of salt. These articles and the milk from their cows, the game caught on the plains, and the fresh water streams furnished them better food and more of it than the immigrants had had in their native land. Mother said the Yankees were lovely people but very wasteful and poor cooks. Their main forte was bread, pies and hotcakes, ham or bacon and eggs. Their vegetables were cooked without taste and their meats either done to death or raw.

As soon as a sufficient number of wagons could be gotten together, that is a hundred or more, they moved off under their respective captain. He headed the train on horseback with his officers, locating camping grounds and selected mornings over fordable streams, directed construction of rafts for carrying men, beast, and wagon over deep waters. Mother tells that after crossing deep streams they had to take off all their clothing and put on a native wrapper, hanging their shoes on the wagon-bob to dry. When they came to a small creek they would wade in it to relieve their feet of the soreness. The dust was terrific in the hot summer and after a rain or thunderstorm the roads were impassable and the poor animals could barely pull their load.

Fording the rivers at times was very difficult. Some rivers were very deep and swift, and often driver and horses were washed down the stream for over a mile. Mother said that often the bottoms of the wagons were filled with water and clothes and provisions would get wet. They would have to rest that day. Take out everything and dry it. After a storm everything was drenched, sagebrush, bunchgrass, and brush. It was almost impossible to make a fire, the smoke would stifle them. They then had to eat bread, raw bacon, and tea. The utensils for cooking were a large iron pot for boiling meat, etc., an iron frying pan, and a skillet for baking bread. The dough was put to it, placed and left on and replenished until the bread was baked. It took about an hour for the bread to be baked.

To each immigrant as he traveled his wagon served as a bedroom, parlor, kitchen, sometimes as a boat. The average day's journey did not exceed thirteen miles, though the trains were in motion from sunrise to sunset, stopping for their midday meal in order to give the animals time to graze. Some caravans consisted of several hundred wagons. Some wagons were drawn by six or eight oxen or horses. Mother said her little team was the envy of the camp. The little mules were never tired and trotted along at a good pace, while often the horses balked and refused to move. It was a grand sight to see this vast train with hundreds of men, women, children, and cattle and wagons going across the desert like a lot of ants. Mother said they were all just like one big family, dividing their joys and sorrows together.

Mother said they did not suffer as many hardships as the previous trains had suffered as they were better provisioned and had less illness and were not molested by the Indians. They had a few dreadful thunderstorms which ruined their food and clothing. Mother's first hardship was the lack of bread. After she ran out of hard tack, and every friend, she found herself without any bread. As she had never baked bread before and was too bashful to ask any of the other women, she decided to try her luck. She put the flour and water in a pan, added some salt, and started to knead it as she had seen the other women do. She worked it an hour until she was tired, covered it over as she had seen the other women do. She left it to stand overnight to raise. Next morning, bright and early she was up, put the dough in the skillet and started her fire.

She piled sagebrush, broomgrass, and buffalo chips below and above and watched it patiently for an hour. All at once she smelled something burning and found it was her bread. It was solid as a rock and black as coal. She was so tired and disheartened she sat down and cried. Her neighbor saw her and asked her what the trouble was. Mother told her. Her neighbor said, "Never mind, I have some nice biscuits and will give you enough for your breakfast, and tonight I will show you how to mix bread. No doubt you forgot the yeast." Mother had no idea that yeast was needed. That evening she was shown how to bake bread, and soon had as nice a bread as any of the women and taught the other women how to make German coffee cake, which she had eaten but never before baked.

FLORA LANGERMAN SPIEGELBERG *was born in 1857 in New York City. In Germany, she met and married Willi Spiegelberg, and in 1875 she arrived in Santa Fe. She died in 1943.*

We traveled, via St. Louis, in very primitive steam cars to West Las Animas, Colorado, which was then the terminus of the railroad. The train arrived at sunset and I was fearfully tired for there were no Pullmans or any riding comforts in those days. Then we continued our journey to Santa Fe for six days and six nights in a stagecoach, drawn by four horses. The stagecoach stopped at the log house coach stations three times daily; an hour to change horses and provide a most primitive meal . . . beans, red or green peppers, coffee and tea without milk or sugar, and occasional delicacies such as buffalo tongues . . . bear and buffalo steaks. I did not relish this food, but my hardened pioneer husband never complained. Many of the stationmasters were old friends of my husband. When they assisted me out of the coach, they raised their big sombreros with a hearty greeting, "Welcome Don Julian and your pretty Tenderfoot Bride of the Santa Fe Trail."

. . . We arrived in Santa Fe on a bright moonlit night. To our great surprise, my husband's brother, Lehman, joined by friends in buggies or on horseback and even on burros, had come to welcome us with a band of Mexican musicians. As the coach drove up the main street accompanied by these friends we were cheered until we reached the home of my husband's brother. There General Devens, Commander of the Territory, waited to welcome us with his military band playing Lohengrin's "Wedding March."

At that time . . . I was one of eight [American] women, fifty American men, officials and merchants, and a Mexican population of two thousand. Amid clean and happy surroundings, I soon forgot all the privations I had endured and I became a satisfied member of the community. . . .

In 1879 I organized the first non-sectarian school for girls in Santa Fe, I rented a room in an old adobe house near the Plaza. It had a mud floor, and to keep it sanitary for the twelve pupils, I disinfected it personally three times weekly. Instead of desks and benches the pupils had little tables and three legged stools. Rev. Dr. Jones, pastor of the Presbyterian Church, engaged a competent teacher from the Presbyterian Mission Society. At my urgent request, before Miss Carpenter accepted the position, I made it obligatory that her pupils be taught to recite the Ten Commandments, and at the same time explain to them that the Ten Commandments are not a religious, but an ethical and moral code upon which civilization rests today. . . .

I also organized the first Children's Gardens; I taught them how cultivate flowers and vegetables . . . gave the children nature study lessons, aided by a magnifying glass. I also taught the children sewing and fancy needlework—each child had her embroidered sampler with her name—and they treasured them.

Our good and tolerant friend Archbishop Lamy always sent us and several other Jewish families gifts of fruit, wines, and flowers as greetings to the Jewish New Year.

Flora's Quilt 2000
94.5 × 76.5 inches

8

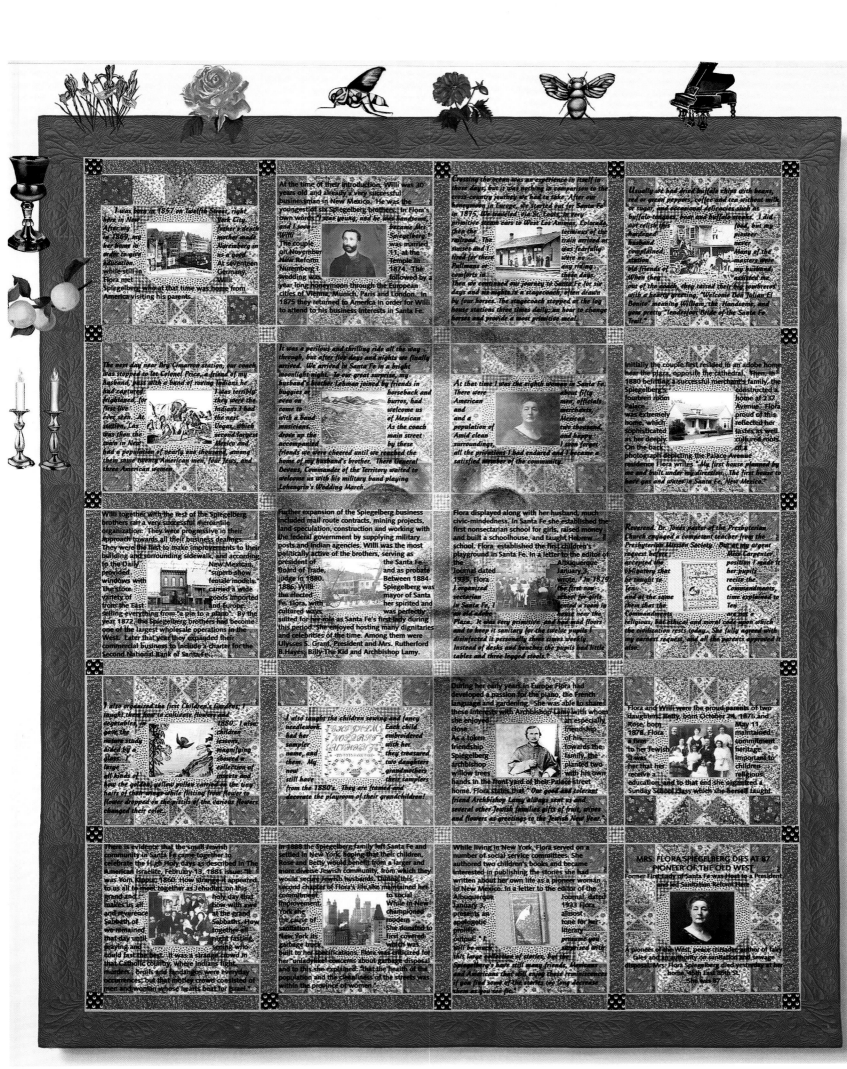

I was born in 1857 on Twelfth Street, right here in New York City. After my father's death in 1869, my mother made her home in Nuremberg in order to give us a good education. At seventeen, while still in Germany, Flora met Willi Spiegelberg who at that time was home from America visiting his parents.

At the time of their introduction, Willi was 30 years old and already a very successful businessman in New Mexico. He was the youngest of six Spiegelberg brothers. In Flora's own words "I was young, and he was handsome, and I soon became Mrs. Willi Spiegelberg." The couple... on November... New Reform... Nuremberg... was married 11, at the... 1874. The wedding was... followed by a year long honeymoon through the European cities of Vienna, Munich, Paris and London. In 1875 they returned to America in order for Willi to attend to his business interests in Santa Fe.

Crossing the ocean was an experience in itself in those days, but it was nothing in comparison to the cross-country journey we had to take. After our honeymoon in Europe, we started out for Santa Fe in 1875. We traveled the St. Louis, in very primitive steam cars to West Los Animas, Colorado, then the... terminus of the railroad. The... train arrived at... houses and I... was fearfully... Pullmans or... any riding comforts in... these days. Then we continued our journey to Santa Fe for six days and six nights in a stagecoach, often drawn by four horses. The stagecoach stopped at the log house stations three times daily: an hour to change horses and provide a most primitive meal.

Usually we had dried buffalo chips with beans, red or green peppers, coffee and tea without milk, or sugar, and occasional delicacies such as buffalo tongues, boot and buffalo steak. I did not relish this... food, but my hardened pioneer husband... Many of the complained... masters were... old friends of... my husband. When they... assisted me out of the coach, they raised their big sombreros with a hearty greeting, "Welcome Don Julian El Benito" meaning William, "the Handsome, and your pretty Tenderfoot Bride of the Santa Fe Trail."

The next day near Dry Cimarron station, our coach was stopped to let Colonel Price, a friend of my husband, pass with a band of roving Indians he had captured. I was terribly frightened, for they were the first live Indians I had ever seen. At... station, Las Vegas, which was then the second-largest town in New Mexico and had a population of nearly ten thousand, among their some twenty American men, four Jews, and three American women.

It was a perilous and thrilling ride all the way through, but after five days and nights we finally arrived. We arrived in Santa Fe in a bright moonlight night. To our great surprise, my husband's brother Lehman joined by friends in buggies or... even on... on horseback and with a band... burros, had come to of musicians... welcome us with a band of Mexican main street... As the coach by these... drove up the... accompanied friends we were cheered until we reached the home of my husband's brother. There General Devens, Commander of the Territory waited to welcome us with his military band playing Lohengrin's Wedding March.

At that time I was the eighth woman in Santa Fe. There were... about fifty American... men, officials and... merchants, and a... Mexican population of... two thousand Amid clean... and happy surroundings... I soon forgot all the privations I had endured and I became a satisfied member of the community.

Initially the couple first resided in an adobe home near the plaza, opposite the cathedral. Then, in 1880 befitting a successful merchant's family, the Spiegelberg's... constructed a fourteen room... home of 237 Palace... Avenue. Flora was extremely... proud of this home, which... reflected her sophisticated... tastes as well as her deeply... cultured roots. On the back of a photograph depicting the Palace Avenue residence Flora writes "My first house planned by me and built under my direction... The first house to have gas and water in Santa Fe, New Mexico."

Willi together with the rest of the Spiegelberg brothers ran a very successful mercantile organization. They were progressive in their approach towards all their business dealings. They were the first to make improvements to their building and surrounding sidewalk, and according to the Daily New Mexican, provided... "superb show windows with... female models." The store... carried a wide variety of... goods imported from the East... and Europe, selling everything from "a pie to a piano." By the year 1872, the Spiegelberg brothers had become one of the largest wholesale operations in the West. Later that year they expanded their commercial business to include a charter for the Second National Bank of Santa Fe.

Further expansion of the Spiegelberg business included mail route contracts, mining projects, and speculation, construction and working with the federal government by supplying military posts and Indian agencies. Willi was the most politically active of the brothers, serving as president of... the Santa Fe Board of Trade, and as probate judge in 1880. Between 1884-1886, Willi the elected mayor of Santa Fe. Flora, with... her spirited and cultured ways... was perfectly suited for her role as Santa Fe's first lady during this period. She enjoyed hosting many dignitaries and celebrities of the time. Among them were Ulysses S. Grant, President and Mrs. Rutherford B. Hayes, Billy The Kid and Archbishop Lamy.

Flora displayed along with her husband, much civic-mindedness. In Santa Fe she established the first nonsectarian school for girls, raised money and built a schoolhouse, and taught Hebrew school. Flora established the first children's playground in Santa Fe. In a letter to the editor of the... Albuquerque Journal dated January 3, 1935, Flora... wrote, "In 1879 I organized the first nonsectarian school for girls in Santa Fe, I rented a room in an old adobe... house near the Plaza. It was very primitive and hot and floors and to keep it sanitary for the twelve pupils I disinfected it personally three times weekly. Instead of desks and benches the pupils had little tables and three legged stools."

Reverend Dr. Jones pastor of the Presbyterian Church engaged a competent teacher from the Presbyterian Mission Society. But at my urgent request before... Miss Carpenter accepted the... position I made it obligatory that... her pupils be taught to... recite the Ten... Commandments, and at the same... time explained to them that the... Ten Commandments are... religious, but ethical and moral code upon which the civilization rests today. She fully agreed with my earnest request, and all the parents approved it also.

I also organized the first Children's Gardens. I taught them how to cultivate flowers and vegetables, in... 1880. I also... took the... children nature study lessons liked by a... magnifying glass. A... showed a huge... collection of... all kinds of... insects and how the golden yellow pollen carried on the way hairs of their wings while flitting from flower to flower dropped on the pistils of the various flowers changed their color.

I also taught the children sewing and fancy needlework. Each child had her sampler, name, and them. My now... still have... two daughters grandmothers... their samplers from the 1880's. They are framed and decorate the playroom of their grandchildren!

During her early years in Europe Flora had developed a passion for the piano, the French language and gardening. She was able to share these interests with Archbishop Lamy with whom she enjoyed... an especially close... friendship. As a token... of his friendship towards the... Spiegelberg family, the archbishop... willow trees planted two with his own hands in the front yard of their Palace Street home. Flora states that "One good and tolerant friend Archbishop Lamy always sent us and several other Jewish families gifts of fruit, wines and flowers as greetings to the Jewish New Year."

Flora and Willi were the proud parents of two daughters: Betty, born October 24, 1876 and Rose, born May 11, 1878. Flora... maintained a firm... commitment to her Jewish... heritage. It was... important to her that her... children receive a... religious education, and to that end she organized a Sunday School class which she herself taught.

There is evidence that the small Jewish community in Santa Fe came together to celebrate the High Holy days as described in The American Israelite, February 19, 1865 issue. "It was Yom Kippur, 1860. How strange it appeared to us all to meet together as Jehudim on this grand and... holy day that makes us all... bow with awe and reverence... at the grand sabbath of... sabbaths. How we remained... together all that day until... night fasting and praying as... strong while... could fast the best. It was a strange crowd in that Catholic country, where Indians fight, murders, brawls and fandangos were everyday occurrences; but that motley crowd consisted of men and women whose hearts beat for Israel."

In 1888 the Spiegelberg family left Santa Fe and settled in New York, hoping that their children, Rose and Betty would benefit from a larger and more diverse Jewish community, from which they would secure Jewish husbands. During this second chapter of Flora's life she maintained her commitment to social improvement. While in New York she... championed the cause of... modern sanitation. She donated to... New York its... first covered garbage truck... which was built to her specifications. Flora was criticized for her "unladylike" concern about garbage disposal and to this she explained, "that the health of the population and the cleanliness of the streets was within the province of women."

While living in New York, Flora served on a number of social service committees. She authored two children's books and became interested in publishing the stories she had written about her own life as a pioneer woman in New Mexico. In a letter to the editor of the Albuquerque Journal, dated January 3, 1933 Flora... presents an apologetic... almost tone for her... prolific literary... output... pronounced until... will be more... this large collection of stories, but the Spiegelberg's have still many friends, Hyman and Andersons that still enjoy these reminiscences if you find some of the stories too long decrease them as best you fit.

MRS. FLORA SPIEGELBERG DIES AT 87 PIONEER OF THE OLD WEST

Former First Lady of Santa Fe was Host to a President and Jeff Sanitation Reformer here...

A pioneer of the West, peace crusader, author of fairy tales and an authority on sanitation and sewage disposal, Mrs. Flora Spiegelberg died yesterday at her home, 439 East 49th St... She was 87...

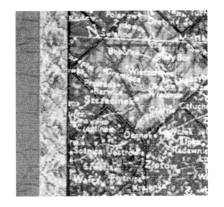

ANNA FREUDENTHAL SOLOMON *was born in a Polish town on the Russian border. She journeyed to the United States with her husband, where they founded Solomonville, Arizona. She died in 1933 at the age of eighty-eight.*

We sold everything we possessed except our three children—Charles, who was three years old, Eva, two, and my youngest daughter Rose, three months old—and started on our journey to New Mexico. We had a very hard trip . . . traveling with those three babies was bad enough, but when we reached La Junta, the end of the railroad in those days, [we] had to travel by stage, packed in like sardines . . . day and night for six days, only stopping to change horses and get something to eat. . . . We stopped over in Santa Fe three days, then we started for Las Cruces, New Mexico, where we had two brothers, Phoebus and Morris, working.

While I was at Las Cruces, my husband looked around for a business opening. After looking around for months he found the place where we are now. At that time it was called Pueblo Viejo.

When we were going to leave Las Cruces we bought a two-seated wagon called a buckboard, and a pair of horses. Into this we put a tent, some bedding, our cooking utensils, our provisions, our clothes, our children, and ourselves. It took us several days and nights to get here. But oh, how often I was frightened thinking that I saw Indians. I did not expect to get here alive with our children. Just before we reached this place, we heard a dreadful noise that Indians make when they are on the warpath. . . . When we were almost home, the Mexicans told us it was a coyote. . . . We arrived here about 12 o'clock at night in August. We slept on the mud floor.

I baked bread from cornmeal for three months in a dutch oven, cooked our meals outdoors like campers do, but I did not mind all that as I could sell goods and the future commenced to look brighter. Still, we had some very dark and sad times. I could not get anyone to help me with my three babies. The worst of all was the washing. I was never used to doing washing. After my second washing I took sick with chills and fever. My baby, Rose also took sick. My husband sent to Fort Grant for the doctor, but the Mexican came back after three days and said he could not get the doctor to come. The chills and fever were dreadful in our place. My baby was sick and I had chills and fever for two years, but that did not hinder us from doing a good business.

We had a contract to deliver charcoal to the Clifton Mining Company, which belonged to my uncle J. Freudenthal and my cousins, Lesinsky, Charles, and Henry. This started our business, and also started the valley. We employed a great many people cutting the mesquite wood, making charcoal, and shipping the same to Clifton by ox teams. . . .

I had my hands full, having at that time five children. The last two were twins, then just a few weeks old. It was impossible for me to take care of Charles, as he was very lively (this is a mild expression). The elder little girls were easier to take care of. . . . Charles got to be a great help to us in the store and in every business transaction. If any child has repaid his parents for their trouble, he certainly has done so, and is a great comfort to us. All of our children have become a great blessing to us.

Anna's Quilt 2000
94 × 77 inches

10

When about two years old my parents told me I was in a trance about half an hour. I woke up out of this for a life full of experience. My parents were not in very good circumstances, but worked themselves up, got to do well, and did a very good business in a very small Polish town adjoining the Russian border. My dear mother was anxious to move to a city where we could have the opportunity of an education. We moved to Krushwitz where my father rented a house and started a business. My parents lost everything in one year. We left Krushwitz for a very small town, with a very few goods, then I was already nine years old. In one year I learned how to read and write in Krushwitz. I then already helped my parents in the store, but things did not change.

My Husband, Isador Solomon came on a visit to his home, his parents living in Krushwitz. Our parents on both sides were old friends. We got acquainted and were married two months after our engagement. My brother Phoebus sent to my parents $2000. Then gave my husband $1000 and the other $1000 was used for wedding and trousseau. The first time I saw my father cry was when I was getting ready to leave home. The wedding was celebrated in a Park Hotel. It was beautiful. My dear mother looked so happy, I will never forget the happy smile on her dear face, but the parting was very sad. When she told me good bye, I knew that I will never see her again.

My sick brother died after I was married. My eldest sister, Henriette was married five years after me. My husband was established in Towanda (Pennsylvania) where he had a business. We lived in Towanda four years, where my three oldest children were born. My oldest son Charles was born in Towanda, my oldest daughter Eva in Mauchang. We lived in Towanda where I was the most homesick person on earth. It was lucky I had my children to take my time up. In the year 1876 (we had gotten married in 1872) business was very dull and my husband told his business to his partner, that is his part. My father wrote to my husband not to open a business in the east, but go to New Mexico. We decided to do so.

We had sold everything we possessed except our three children, Charles who was three years old, Eva was two years, and my youngest daughter Rose three months old, and started on our journey to New Mexico. We had a very hard trip; even on the railroad traveling with those three babies was bad enough, but when we reached La Junta, the end of the railroad in those days, we had to travel by stage packed in like sardines, traveling day and night for six days; only stopped to change horses and get something to eat like chile con carne and frijoles. I forgot to mention that we stopped over in Santa Fe three days, then we started for Las Cruces, New Mexico where we had our two brothers, Phoebus and Morris. When we got there I was tired out to death.

When we were going to leave Las Cruces we bought a two seated wagon called a buckboard, and a pair of horses. Into this we put a tent, some bedding, our kitchen utensils, our provisions, our clothes, our children and ourselves. It took us several days and nights to get here. But oh, how frightened I was thinking that I saw Indians. I did not expect to get here alive with our children. Just before we reached this place, we heard a dreadful noise that Indians make when they are on the warpath. It was a beautiful night, I remember it as if it was last night. When we were almost home, the Mexicans told us that it was a Coyote, as the Indians make the same peculiar noise.

While I was at Las Cruces, my husband was looking around for a business opening. After looking around for four months he found a place near where we are now. At that time it was called Pueblo Viejo. Sending our most necessary things for a seven days trip on that buckboard, as bedding and cooking utensils and a tent to sleep nights. When we finally got to our place our town consisted of four little Mexican huts or ranchos, our house, the largest of these stood in the center of the plaza. After living there about three months our wagons with goods from Las Cruces arrived. What a happy day that was, until then we had no bed to sleep in, no stove to cook on, no table to eat off, no flour to bake bread.

We arrived here about twelve o'clock at night in August. We slept on the mud floor. My husband woke me up to show me some Indians that were here on passes from San Carlos reservation. I had never seen an Indian before. Now we had to start housekeeping, no furniture, no cooking stove and nothing else that belongs to the comfort of the human race. We cooked outdoors on the ground; we had a stove and other necessary things coming from Las Cruces sent by ox teams with two loads of goods for our store that we were going to put up, but the wagon had dropped down on the road and we had to send someone to repair them. They got here after being three months on the road.

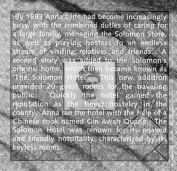

I baked bread out of cornmeal for three months in a dutch oven, cooked meals outdoors like campers do, but I did not mind all that, as I could sell goods and the future commenced to look a little brighter. Still we had some very dark and sad times. I could not get anyone to help me with my three babies. The worst of all was the washing. After my second washing I took sick with chills and fever. My baby Rose also took sick. My husband sent for the doctor at Fort Grant, but the Mexican came back after three days and said he could not get the doctor to come. The chills and fever were dreadful in our place. My baby was sick and I had chills and fever for two years, but that did not hinder us from doing a good business.

We had a contract of delivering charcoal to the Clifton Mining Co. which belonged to my uncle J. Freudenthal and my cousins Lesinsky, Charles and Henry. This started our business and also started the valley. We employed a great many people, cutting the wood, making charcoal and shipping it to Clifton by ox teams. This took a great deal of hard work to oversee it and mind it. I could not get any decent person to help me. My husband attended the outdoors work and I attended the store and housework. We also started building; at first a bedroom, then a store. I felt like the Queen of England when that store was finished. We kept on building right around the old house.

I had my hands full at that time, having at that time five children, Eva, Rose, Harry and Lillie. The last two were twins, then just a few weeks old. It was impossible then for me to take care of Charles, as he was very lively (this is a very mild expression.) The elder little girls were easier to take care of. Charles got to be a great help to us in the store and in every business transaction. If any child has repaid his parents for their trouble, he certainly has done so, and is still a great comfort to us. All of our children have become a great blessing to us. Frieda Mashbir (Anna's sister) joined Anna and Isadore in Solomonville helping out in the store and becoming in 1906 postmaster of Solomonville. Having additional family nearby helped Anna to retain the families Jewish identity. They observed Passover, celebrated at Chanukah and closed the store on Yom Kippur.

By 1883 Anna's life had become increasingly busy, with the combined duties of caring for a large family, managing the Solomon Store, as well as playing hostess to an endless stream of visiting relatives and friends. A second story was added to the Solomon's original home, which then became known as The Solomon Hotel. This new addition provided 20 guest rooms for the traveling public. Quickly the hotel gained the reputation as the finest hostelry in the county. Anna ran the hotel with the help of a Chinese cook named Gin Awah Quang. The Solomon Hotel was renown for its relaxed and friendly hospitality, characterized by its keyless rooms.

The Solomon Hotel was the hub of the town's activity. The hotel was strictly Anna's domain. Anna utilized the fresh fruits and vegetables that were grown in her orchard across the road from the hotel. The meats that were served were wagoned in from the Solomon ranch. Continental pastries were prepared in the kitchen under Anna's watchful eye.

The Solomon Hotel was located on the northwest corner of Bowie and Main streets. The buildings were territorial in style, and had a portal which wrapped around its exterior.

In 1886 the Warm Springs Apaches were driven into Mexico, and the Chiricahua deported to Florida. These events diminished the daily threat to life and property in Solomonville. For the first time the citizens of the town were able to focus less on defense, and more upon reaching their goal of aspiring to become the leading financial, administrative, and agricultural trade center between El Paso and Tucson.

Anna continued with great success to run both The Solomon Commercial Store, and The Solomon Hotel. During this period, Anna also provided a quality education designed to suit the individual needs of each of her six children.

When Charles was thirteen years old I took him to Demopolis. Adolph Solomon wanted me to take him to his sister, where his sister's children went to school. On our way home Charles and I went to the White House in Washington, also the Capital and everything else that was worth seeing, and carrying Blanche on my arm. When we got home we took Charles to Belmont on Mt. Lilienthal's advice. He went to New York to business college. After he returned from there he got to be a great help to us in business and in everything else. I never will forget when Charles and I got dressed up for the first masquerade ball at Solomonville.

The Solomon children were deeply involved in the community of Solomonville. They lived in the hotel, attended the local primary school and helped out in both the store and the hotel. Around the age of fourteen Blanche and Lillie were sent to New York to attend Miss Well's Boarding School.

Anna insisted that all her children marry within the Jewish faith. To this end she often enlisted the aid of her son Charles who acting in the role of shadchan, or matchmaker traveled the surrounding states looking for suitable husbands for his sisters. This task was accomplished in every case. In 1896 a double ring ceremony was held for Eva and Rose. Eva wed Julius Wetzler and Rosa married David Goldberg of Phoenix.

By 1915 Anna and Isadore had retired. The Solomon Commercial Company was sold in 1916, and the hotel in 1919. Their retirement plans consisted of spending more time with their children and living in a moderate climate. They spent their final decade together in Los Angeles, an experience which Anna relished. Isadore on the other hand lamented his departure from his beloved Solomonville. In 1922 Anna and Isadore celebrated their 50th wedding anniversary.

The population of Solomonville continued to shrink after the Solomon's departure. Those who remained, lasted only until a series of droughts forced them to sell out. By 1950 the town's name was shortened to Solomon.

Pioneer Woman Of Solomonville
Dies In California City
May 12, 1933
Mrs. Anna Solomon, widow of the founder of Solomonville, died in San Deigo California, Thursday of last week and was interred Saturday in the Hollywood Mausoleum. Mrs. Solomon came to Graham county with her husband in 1876. They established and conducted for many years the Hotel Solomon and a general store. She was 88 years old at the time of her death. Surviving sons and daughters are Harry Solomon, Mrs. Blanche Weinberger, and Mrs. Julius Wetzler.

SARAH THAL *was born in Ellingen, Germany. She arrived in the United States in 1882 to homestead land in Dodds Township, North Dakota.*

I had never seen frame houses until we reached America. Everything I saw from the train window was interesting and new. We reached Grand Forks late at night. Being unable to speak English I could not make my wants known so I went to bed without supper. I reached Larimore hungry but safely. Here I met my husband. He was wearing a buffalo skin coat, the first I had ever seen. With him was Sol Mendelson, the manager of the Sam Thal farm.

A newcomer must be of course experiencing much embarrassment. My worst one day was when Mr. Mendelson brought in a crate of pork and asked me, a piously reared Jewess, to cook it. In time I consented. However, I never forgot my religious teachings. In the spring of 1883 we homesteaded land in Dodds Township along the supposed railroad right of way. Here we planted our first garden. My, how I loved to watch things grow in that newly broken land.

That fall, I would look out of the window and see fires in the distance. These I believed were far off factories. I was still unable to realize the completeness of our isolation. That fall my second baby, Jacob, was born. I was attended by a Mrs. Saunders, an English woman. It was in September. The weather turned cold and the wind blew from the North. It found its way through every crack in that poorly built house. I was so cold that during the first night they moved my bed into the living room by the stove and pinned sheets around it to keep the draft out and so I lived through the first childbirth in the prairies. I liked to think that God watched out for us poor lonely women when the stork came.

In the spring our baby was taken very ill. I wanted a doctor so badly. There was a terrific storm and when it cleared the snow was ten feet deep. My husband couldn't risk a trip to Larimore. On the fourth day my baby died unattended. I never forgave the prairies for that. He was buried in the lot with Mrs. Seliger and a child of the Mendelson's. For many years we kept up the lonely graves. In time the wolves and elements destroyed them. They are unmarked in all save my memory.

All the women in the neighborhood, save two, lived to see their children grow up. Mrs. Fahey died, leaving seven, the eldest fifteen. By this time most of the sod houses and barns had been replaced by frame buildings, and such luxuries as buggies and driving horses became common.

There were schools in every district. Then came hanging lamps, upholstered furniture, carpets and curtains, and when the cream separator came into common use I felt that the pioneer's days were gone and that the land was tamed forever. Year by year wild ducks and geese became scarcer, the storms became fewer and less severe and the Northern Lights less mysterious.

Sarah's Quilt 2001
104 × 104 inches
quilting assistance: Cindy Barfield, Amy Varner

SOPHIE TRUPIN *was born in Seltz, Russia, in 1903, arrived in the United States in 1908, and died in 1992.*

I remember the morning when we started on the last lap of our journey to the home my father had built for us. My mother sat with my father on the bench that ran across the front of the wagon, and we children sat in the wagon box amidst the baggage and provisions.

We traveled all day, and I don't remember meeting any other wagon or stopping anywhere. There were no houses or trees or rivers, only prairies and hills and sky. To my mother it must have been fearsome and devastating to be plunged into this vast, empty world after knowing only the narrow confines of her familiar ghetto.

My mother carried only three *mitzvoth*; that is all that is expected of a Jewish woman. But in reality she could carry only two of the three. In her baggage were the four brass candlesticks which she polished every Friday at sundown from the day she was married, fulfilling the first *mitzvah*. The second mitzvah, as she taught me, was to say a blessing over the piece of dough she tossed into the fire when she was baking the Sabbath loaves. The third mitzvah, immersion in the ritual bath once every month, she could not carry with her.

My mother kept a kosher home, observing every holiday. This was never easy, but here it was even harder than it had been in the Old Country. There was no kosher meat, and hard-working men needed nourishment, so my father learned how to slaughter fowl in the prescribed way. He had a special ritual knife for this purpose and made a special prayer. I remember seeing my mother make Chanukah candles. I don't know what she used to make them, but they were orange, and I used to look at these candles hanging from the rafters in the woodshed.

Our family never worked on the Sabbath. There was nothing unusual about this in the Old World; any other mode of living was unthinkable. The Sabbath was considered even holier than any of the major holidays. Thus it was on the Sabbath day, in any season, my father and brothers devoted themselves to the study of Holy Writ. There was no synagogue or minyan of ten, but no matter.

Each morning the *tefillen* was wound about the arm, and the forehead was adorned with the small black box containing the ancient prayer offered up to God, as it had been for centuries.

The Holy Days were observed with prayers, special dishes which my mother prepared, and cessation from work. However, for the Day of Atonement, Yom Kippur, something special had to be done. Even those Jews who had not spent their Sabbaths in rest and study and contemplation were compelled to stop and remember their training. And so it came about that on the day preceding Yom Kippur all the Jewish homesteaders, who were scattered over many miles, gathered their families and started on a journey to a common meeting place in order to observe the holiest day of the year. The farmhouse that could accommodate the most worshippers was the house of the Weinbergs. It was to be our shul.

Sophie's Quilt 2000
90 × 90 inches
quilting assistance: Cindy Barfield, Amy Varner
Courtesy of the Autry Museum of Western Heritage.

Not part of the traveling exhibition.

The voyage from America seemed endless, and the world of water that engulfed us was terrifying. We spent most of our time below deck in what must have been the steerage section. It was a dimly lit, low ceilinged room, quite large and round, with bunks built into the walls. Each family occupied a section of upper and lower bunks. After a long voyage across the ocean the journey began all over again, but this time along endless miles of railroad tracks. Somewhere in this vast country was a place called "Nordakota." I had heard that strange name again and again for as long as I could remember. That was where our traveling would come to an end. I remember the scratchy, plush seats of these quimsy trains, and the perpetual jolting and jostling.

Then we were traveling westward once more. We must have presented a strange picture with our foreign clothes and battered baggage. I imagine we appeared like a tableau, titled "A Jewish Immigrant Mother and Her Children." The central figure, a young, slight woman with a shawl draped across her shoulders; two young boys with caps and pages, or earlocks, standing beside her; and two little girls in front with bundles at their feet. We spoke no English.

I remember the morning when we started on the last lap of our journey to the home my father had built for us. My mother sat with my father on the bench that ran across the front of the wagon, and we children sat in the wagon box amidst the baggage and provisions. We traveled all day, and I don't remember meeting any other wagon or stopping anywhere. There were no houses or trees or rivers, only prairies and hills and sky. To my mother it must have been fearsome and devastating to be plunged into this vast, empty world after knowing only the narrow confines of her familiar ghetto.

My mother carried only three mitzvot; that is all that is expected of a Jewish woman. But in reality she could carry only two of the three. In her baggage were the four brass candlesticks which she polished every Friday at sundown from the day she was married, fulfilling the first mitzvah. The second mitzvah, as she taught me, was to say a blessing over the piece of dough she tossed into the fire when she was baking the Sabbath loaves. The third mitzvah, immersion in the ritual bath once every month, she could not carry with her.

My mother kept a kosher home, observing every holiday. This was never easy, but here it was even harder than it had been in the Old Country. There was no kosher meat, and hard-working men needed nourishment, so my father learned how to slaughter fowl in the prescribed way. He had a special ritual knife for this purpose and made a special prayer. I remember seeing my mother make Chanukah candles. I don't know what she used to make them with, but they were orange, and I used to look at these candles hanging from the rafters in the woodshed.

Several days before Passover, when the melting snow had run into the narrow valley at the south side of the hill we lived on, my mother, sister, and I set about getting our home ready for the holiday. Mother whitewashed off the walls and scoured the floors. She made the utensils kosher for Passover with scalding hot water. A stone was first heated in the range until it was red hot. It was then put into a very large pot of boiling water, making the water sizzle and hiss. The utensils were boiled for some time in this water. In addition every piece of furniture was carried down to the slou and scrubbed and allowed to dry on the bank where the young grass was just beginning to appear.

Our family never worked on the Sabbath. There was nothing unusual about this in the Old World; any other mode of living was unthinkable. The Sabbath was considered even holier than any of the major holidays. Thus it was on the Sabbath day, in any season, my father and brothers devoted themselves to the study of Holy Writ. There was no synagogue or minyan of ten, but no matter. Each morning the tefillin was wound about the arm, and the forehead was adorned with the small black box containing the ancient prayer offered up to God, as it had been for centuries.

The Holy Days were observed with prayers, special dishes which my mother prepared, and cessation from work. However, for the Day of Atonement, Yom Kippur, something special had to be done. Even those Jews who had not spent their Sabbaths in rest, study and contemplation were compelled to stop and remember their training. And so it came about that on the day preceding Yom Kippur all the Jewish homesteaders, who were scattered over many miles, gathered their families and started on a journey to a common meeting place in order to observe the holiest day of the year. The farmhouse that could accommodate the most worshipers was the house of the Weinberg's. It was to be our shul.

BETTY SPIEGELBERG *married Levi Spiegelberg in 1848, and arrived in Santa Fe in the 1860s. Her story is narrated by her sister-in-law, Flora Spiegelberg.*

My brother-in-law Levi's wife was young and very beautiful. Their only pleasant recreation was a buggy ride every Sunday to visit the nearby Indian pueblos and watch them mold pottery and make gold and silver jewelry. One Sunday as they drove past General Sibley's headquarters they noticed that some of the officers and soldiers arose and stared at them. The following day an old pioneer friend told Levi, "When you drove past military headquarters Sunday, I overheard this remark, 'By Gringo! What a beautiful woman in these war times. A fellow might be tempted to kidnap her.'"

To protect his wife, Levi's three brothers slept in an adjoining room with loaded guns to ward off any attempt to kidnap her. My brother-in-law forbade his wife even to look out of her bedroom window. One day she heard a woman crying and moaning under her window, "For God's sake, help me! I am starving and bleeding to death." Remembering her husband's warning, she ran across the yard into the store to call him, but it was full of soldiers shouting and fighting for provisions.

She rushed back to her room, and when the crying and pitiful appeals continued, she could not resist any longer and looked out of the window and saw a young Negro girl, who begged for help. Assisted by her Mexican maid, she dragged the girl into the house, washed and fed her, and sent for a doctor.

The girl had been stolen from her master's plantation by General Sibley's soldiers, assaulted, and abused by them. The Spiegelberg brothers not only bought her freedom, but also freed a man slave and adopted an Indian girl the Confederate soldiers had captured.

Betty's Quilt 2000
84 × 82.5 inches

The following excerpt is from Flora Spiegelberg's 'Reminiscences of a Jewish Bride On The Santa Fe Trail' written in August of 1937. In this story, Flora writes about her sister-in-law Betty Spiegelberg's adventures in Santa Fe, circa 1874. Betty arrived in Santa Fe in the early 1860's after taking the railroad to the end of Missouri and then traveling up the steep Santa Fe Trail by ox train.

My brother-in-law Levi's wife was young and very beautiful and at that time was the fifth American woman in Santa Fe. Their only pleasant recreation was a buggy ride every Sunday to visit the nearby Indian pueblos and watch them mold pottery and gold and silver jewelry. One Sunday as they drove past General Sibley's headquarters, they noticed that some of the officers arose and stared at them. The following day an old pioneer friend told Levi: "When you drove past military headquarters Sunday, I overheard this remark: 'By Gringo! What a beautiful woman in these wartimes. A fellow might be tempted to kidnap her.'"

To protect his wife, Levi's three brothers slept in an adjoining room with loaded guns to ward off any attempt to kidnap her. My brother-in-law forbid his wife even to look out of her bedroom window, but one day she heard a woman crying and moaning under her window: "For God's sake, help me! I am starving and bleeding to death." Remembering her husband's warning, she ran across the yard into the store to call him, but it was full of soldiers shouting and fighting for provisions.

So, she rushed back to her room, and when the crying and pitiful appeals continued, she could not resist any longer and looked out of the window and saw a young Negro girl who begged for help. Assisted by her Mexican maid, she dragged her into the house, washed and fed her, and sent for a doctor. The girl had been stolen from her master's plantation by General Sibley's soldiers, assaulted and abused by them. The Spiegelberg brothers not only bought her freedom, but also a man slave and adopted an Indian girl and boy the Confederate soldiers had captured.

MRS. ZELICKSON *arrived in Canada in 1891 and settled in Hirsch, Saskatchewan. In 1925 she responded to an ongoing discussion in the magazine* Nor'-West Farmer *on the topic of what a woman's work was worth.*

Being a pioneer of Southern Saskatchewan, it is quite interesting to note the value of work which I have performed. Although not having the money in cash, I figure the experience is worth it. I am one of the oldest pioneers in Southern Saskatchewan, coming to this country in 1891 and settling with my husband in our present location in 1892. Having worked here for thirty-three years you will see in the latter part of this letter what I have done. On remarking the value of my work, I do not reckon it the wage of a maid but I figure it as taking the produce to market. . . . I estimate the value of my work for these thirty-five years as $141,578. I have cooked 361,351 meals, baked 78,800 loaves of bread, 12,045 cakes, 5,158 pies, preserved 3,300 quarts of fruit, churned 13,728 pounds of butter and raised 4,950 poultry. I have put in 48,180 hours scrubbing, cleaning, and washing. I think this is quite a record and will be pleased to hear from any woman who can beat it.

Mrs. Zelickson's Quilt 2001
94.5 × 78 inches
quilting assistance: Cindy Barfield, Amy Varner

"Being a
pioneer of
Southern Saskatchewan,
it is quite interesting to note
the value of work which I have
performed. Although not having the money
in cash, I figure the experience is worth it. I am
one of the oldest pioneers in Southern Saskatchewan,
coming to this country in 1891 and settling with my husband in
my present location in 1892. Having worked here for 33 years you will
see in the latter part of this letter what I have done. On remarking on the
value of my work I do not reckon it the wage of a maid but I figure it as taking the
produce to market . . . I estimate the value of my work for these 35 years as
$141,578. I have cooked 361,351 meals, baked 78,800 loaves of
bread, 12,045 cakes, 5,158 pies, preserved 3,300 quarts of
fruit, churned 13,728 pounds of butter and raised 4,950
poultry. I have put in 48,180 hours scrubbing,
cleaning and washing. I think this is quite a
record and will be pleased to hear
from any woman who can
beat it."

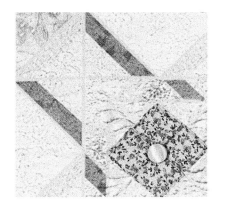

RACHEL BELLA CALOF *was born in Russia in 1876. She arrived in Devil's Lake, North Dakota, in 1894 as a mail-order bride for Abraham Calof. She died in Seattle, Washington, in 1954.*

The law provided that a homestead claim could be filed as late as five years from the time a homesteader settled on the land, but I had only the six weeks before my marriage in which to file my claim. Married women whose husbands owned or were claiming land were denied homestead claim rights, but single women had the same rights as men. Abraham's land would be in his name but mine would be in my maiden name.

Finally the day came. The wedding, my friends, was a knockout. Since Abraham's niece, Doba, had the largest home with two rooms, she offered her palace for the occasion. My soon to be in-laws, spreading their usual cheer and good will, insisted that the bride and groom had to fast until the ceremony was completed. I was instructed to say my prayers with tears and to implore my dead parents, or at least my departed mother, to attend my wedding.

My bridal gown, which I had made myself, was of yellow, blue, and white stripes. Abraham's suit hung so low in the back that it might have passed for what is today called "tails." Those in attendance were Abraham's family, and his nieces, Doba and Sarah, their husbands, and their two children. Our wedding gifts were a red felt tablecloth with green flowers, two chickens, and from Charlie and Faga two short women's undershirts. A delayed gift of some little chicks was also promised for next spring by one of the nieces.

All brides remember their wedding ceremony and mine was truly memorable. I was seated in a chair. Abraham was given a flour sack which he was instructed to place over my face. Well, at least one could cry in private under the cover.

Being effectively blinded, I was now led to the *huppah* (wedding canopy) by Doba and her husband.

The huppah was built of a shawl tied to four sticks. The music was provided by the singing of the women while the men beat time on tin pans.

Following the ceremony the table was set and we sat down to a truly magnificent banquet, which consisted of beans, rice with raisins, chicken soup, and roast chicken. The flour sack had been replaced by a handkerchief bound over my eyes. I wanted to remove it to at least be present at my own marriage, but my mother-in-law was quick to forbid it. I did not want to create a scene at my own wedding and so I submitted to these primitive customs.

The festivities over, bride and groom started home, and in short order, even before my wedding day was over, I was cruelly thrust back into the reality of my life. I learned that the Calof men had decided prior to my marriage that Abe and I must share our home with others for the entire coming winter, and therefore, Abe's father, mother, and brother Moses would double up with us for the coming months.

In an instant, the happiness of my marriage turned to bitterness. The knowledge that I was to spend my honeymoon in a tiny space shared with three strangers was more than I could bear. I hoped death would take me now, that I would not reach home alive. But my fervent wish was not granted, and it was life, not death, with which I had to cope.

Rachel's Quilt 2001
103 × 103 inches
quilting assistance: Cindy Barfield, Amy Varner

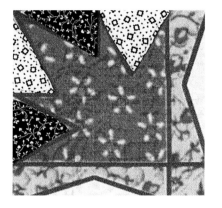

ANNA MARKS *was born in Russian-occupied Poland in 1847. She married Wolff Marks in 1862, and in 1880 they moved to Eureka City, a rich mining area south of Salt Lake City, Utah. Her story is told by Sam F. Elton and Beth K. Harris.*

In the early days of Tintic . . . two men, John O. Freckleton and Hyrum Gardner, claimed the land in the west end of Pinion Canyon. They opened the first road through Pinion Canyon. They placed a toll gate in the narrow part of the canyon charging a fee for all who entered. A Jewish lady, Anna Marks, and her husband, Wolff, hearing of the opportunities in Tintic, proceeded up Pinion Canyon with their outfit. She was in the lead in a buggy, followed by many wagons loaded with everything necessary to open a store. When she came to the gate she refused to pay the toll. A verbal war was on, the air turning blue with Anna's cuss words. She summoned her bodyguard and with guns drawn they tore down the tollgate and went on to Eureka. Anna took possession of some ground on the south side of the street and was soon in business. Her right to the ground was hotly contested by a man named Pat Shay. Many verbal arguments followed. Finally she pulled her guns on Pat. He went flying and so did the bullets. He made it to a pile of posts. He wasn't hit, but she sure made the bark fly. From then on no one crossed Anna Marks. . . .

Anna Marks's reputation for being the feistiest woman in the state was built solidly on many similar reports. An outstanding example of her feuding occurred when she carried on a historic battle with the Denver and Rio Grande, holding up the building of a railroad at gunpoint until the Denver and Rio Grande met her price to cross the section of her land.

Anna Marks died of a heart attack in Eureka City on April 19, 1912.

Anna Marks's Quilt 2001
100 × 98 inches

Anna Rich Marks was born in Russian-occupied Poland on March 15, 1847. While the pogroms raged in Europe, Anna decided to move to London, England. Here she met and married Wolff Marks in 1862 when she was only 15 years old. Not long after their wedding, the couple set off for America to seek their fortune. While in New York, Anna and Wolff became intrigued by the stories they heard of the rich mining towns in the West.

For several years Anna and Wolff operated a store in Salt Lake City. Then, in 1880 they decided to move to Eureka City, a rich Tintic mining area, located approximately 60 miles south of Salt Lake City. While living in Eureka City, Anna gained a reputation for being the feistiest woman in the state. A local historian, Sam F. Elton, described Anna's arrival in the Eureka area in the following way:

"In the early days of Tintic ... two men, John O. Freckleton and Hyrum Gardner claimed the land in the west end of Pinion Canyon. They placed a toll gate in the narrow part of the canyon charging a fee for all who entered.

A Jewish lady, Anna Marks and her husband, Wolff, hearing of the opportunities in Tintic, proceeded up Pinion Canyon with their outfit. She was in the lead in a buggy followed by many wagons loaded with everything necessary to open a store. A verbal war was on, the air turning blue with Anna's cuss words. She summoned . her bodyguard and with guns drawn they tore down the toll gate and went on to Eureka.

Anna took possession of some ground on the south side of the street and was soon in business. Her right to the ground was hotly contested by a man named Pat Shay. Many verbal arguments followed. Finally she pulled her guns on Pat. He went flying and so did the bullets. He made it to a pile of posts. He wasn't hit, but she sure made the bark fly. From then on no one crossed Anna Marks."

1. Sam F. Elton, The Eureka Reporter, October 25, 1963, p. 7.

Anna Marks' reputation for being the most feisty woman in the state, was built solidly upon many similar reports. An outstanding example of her feuding occurred when " she carried on a historic battle with the Denver and Rio Grande, holding up the building of a railroad at gunpoint until the Rio Grande met her price to cross the section of her land." [2]
Anna Marks died of a heart attack in Eureka City on April 19, 1912.

2. Beth Kay Harris, Towns of Tintic (Denver, 1961), p. 69.

ANDREA KALINOWSKI
INTERVIEWED BY ALINE CHIPMAN BRANDAUER

Born in Montreal in 1953, Andrea Wexler Kalinowski established herself as a free-thinking and talented young artist. After apprenticing with ceramicist Rosalie Naimer, she went on to attend the Sheridan College of Applied Arts and Technology in Toronto, then the Nova Scotia College of Art in Halifax, where she received a B.F.A. in 1975. While at Nova Scotia, Kalinowski studied with some of the best painters of her generation: artists Eric Fischl and Mira Schor. Kalinowski helped establish the Art Therapy Program at the psychiatric unit of Montreal's Jewish General Hospital, and then went on to Hahnemann Medical School in Philadelphia, where she graduated with a Master's Degree in Creative Arts Therapy. After spending six years working at the Philadelphia Psychiatric Hospital and the Southern Home for Children in Philadelphia, she decided to devote her time to painting. Since 1986 the artist has lived in Santa Fe, New Mexico, with her husband and two children. —A.C.B.

BRANDAUER: **How did you choose Jewish pioneer women as your subject for this body of work?**

KALINOWSKI: As a Jewish girl growing up in the fifties and sixties in Montreal, Canada, I always felt different, set apart. These feelings stemmed from being an Anglo in a French community, and a Jew in a powerfully Catholic province. Also, I was a female without an equal voice.

This outsider experience challenged, exhausted, and eventually prepared me to tell the stories of other Jewish women from another place and time, who also found themselves set apart.

I wondered about Jewish women who had pioneered the trails of the West. I wanted to know more about them. What compelling reasons drove them to such bravery and willingness to stray from their familiar lives, to endure hardships? How did these women have an impact on the isolated territory in which they found themselves? How did they shape the lives of their families and their larger communities?

The voices and faces of these early Jewish pioneer women captured my heart and imagination.

Can you describe the work you did leading up to this?

Five years ago I was painting large canvases depicting movie billboards from India. The content of the work consisted of romantic and idealized imagery, usually of a woman beautifully coiffed gazing into the dark eyes of a "Clark Gable" love interest. I'm not exactly sure why I felt compelled to paint these images. Probably, it was the poignant contrast between the highly stylized imagery and the extreme poverty existing in the streets below the signs themselves. One thing I know for sure, the subject matter of these paintings helped further my interest in the woman's role, both within familial boundaries and in broader contexts.

Next came a series of paintings depicting Chinese women surrounded by the symbols that illustrated the fundamental themes of their lives, such as family, education, adornment, and community.

About three years ago I entered a juried art show and I submitted three entries from the series, *Chinese Women*. Two of the paintings were rejected and one accepted. I asked myself, why weren't all of the paintings accepted?

I was able to track down the juror for the show and through our conversation I gained a new perspective and direction for my work. She said, "You paint beautifully, but a lot of artists paint beautifully." Specifically, she helped me to identify that my own cultural history was rich and diverse and probably held the key to the direction my artwork would take.

This realization led me to broaden my awareness of Jewish women's history. I began by scouring various Jewish archives, university libraries, and state historical societies across the country to see what new information I could gather. My deepest hope was to encounter the writing of Jewish women who, like myself, had spent time in their lives being disconnected from their Jewish roots in one way or another. This led me toward research that uncovered diaries, memoirs, and letters written by Jewish women who were part of the larger story of the effort toward western expansion.

From the beginning, Jewish women were among those who pioneered the West, served their country through times of war, and were actively engaged in the women's movement. I have come to know, through research, that Jewish women have always been present and have always played an important role in the history of this country.

Why did you incorporate quilting into these artworks?

Having been a painter for the past twenty years, I initially felt I should be utilizing the brush and paint in these works. Like many developments in the creative process, the idea of using quilting, and other women to assist in the quilting process, occurred later. The earliest works in the series do have hand-painted images of symbols that characterize the story. For instance, Flora Spiegelberg's story mentions that in 1880 she organized the first Children's Garden in Santa Fe. Here she taught the children how to grow vegetables and study nature with the aid of a magnifying glass. On *Flora's Quilt* you'll find hand-painted lemons, flowers, and butterflies symbolic of that time in her life. A small amount of quilting appears on this piece as well, but as this was an early work in the series, the actual quilting was an afterthought.

Soon I began to think that quilting was a more natural and inherently more honest application to the artwork. It provided a way for the creative process to be shared, bringing in members of the community, similar to the way that quilts had provided community, sisterhood, and comfort during these pioneer women's lives. Also, it's wonderful to be able to incorporate a range of techniques—these quilts are initially designed digitally, then hand-worked for about twenty hours each.

How does the history of the quilt relate to the history of women in this country?

Throughout the nineteenth century women used their quilts as fabrics on which to inscribe not only a personal but a public narrative. The quilts registered their responses to, and participation in, major social, economic, and political developments of the time. The quilt has long been associated with opposition to political repression. Quilts were used by the Underground Railroad to help escaping slaves make their way from the South to the northern states—guiding them to "safe houses on this trail." During the Temperance Movement quilts served as banners, petitions, and fund-raising tools, and were hung in many a meeting hall where women gathered for reform efforts. Quilts have been used in various ways to expand women's roles.

On the westward journey itself, quilts lined the wagons making them, as one woman wrote, "impervious to wind and weather." Quilts were used to wrap fragile china and to pad the sides of wagons during Indian attacks. They were used to bury the dead . . . there were many stretches of desert and plains on the trail West where no wood was available so quilts were used instead of coffins. During the wagon trips women brought with them work baskets with sewing materials for spare moments. They visited from wagon to wagon tatting, quilting, knitting, and exchanging recipes. Sewing served as a reassurance of the women's civilized female identity.

It was extremely important for women in the West to create female support systems in the newly settled areas. Homes, farms, could easily be twenty to thirty miles from each other. Women especially suffered from this social isolation. Men had more mobility —making trips for supplies or to trade—and were often absent from the home for weeks at a time. The necessity for warm bedding brought women together, and needlework skills became a primary form of bonding.

For me, the quilt design acts as a backbone—a structure into which a multitude of historical texts and images can be gathered and easily accessed. I use the quilt structure as a way of keeping the work an integrated whole.

The artist Sabra Moore comes from a Texan family of quilt makers. She said recently, "When I look at a quilt, specifically when I look at a quilt from my family, I know exactly who made it, whose dresses and suits every little scrap came from. There's an emotional charge because of that connection."

I think I share a similar emotional connection. It's important to let these pioneer women speak for themselves, and to allow these stories to remain as "intact" as possible. After all, real history is encapsulatedin these quilts. It's important for me to remain vigilant in terms of sharing and exposing the reality of these women's lives . . . their joys, disappointments, frustrations, and successes are the "scraps" that become the fabric from which a new and broader understanding can evolve.

Since my goal in this work is to stay true to the history, I am especially conscious not to utilize it as a mere element of the artwork but rather as the soul of the work itself. One of the challenges is to decide which aspects of the story to leave in and which to take out. Often there is a story within the larger one. Needless to say, there are many common elements among the memoirs, such as fear of starvation, child-loss, and the struggle to maintain Jewish customs and rituals on the primitive prairie. There's an intricate balance that needs to be maintained when trying to create something aesthetically pleasing, historically correct, and at the same time approachable.

What fragments of someone's life do you decide to portray?

A good example is the story Fanny Sharlip tells when she writes about the devastation of rising anti-Semitism in her small town of Borosna, Russia. She begins by recalling a nearly perfect, upper-class childhood, with vivid memories of the samovar constantly being refilled and servants busy providing generous portions of preserves, tea, and cake. Then Fanny continues by detailing how the anti-Semitic climate of the era slowly erodes the stability of her almost fairytale existence.

Fanny Sharlip shares with us, on a deeply personal level, the fears her family faces as the anti-Semitic acts increase in regularity and severity. When the windows of her father's business are broken the family comes to realize they must finally leave Russia. Next, Fanny describes the sea voyage she, her mother, and six siblings take to join her father. Fanny's diary continues on to describe her life in the United States, working in a clothing factory in Philadelphia, her marriage to Ben Sharlip, and lastly, her life in Los Angeles where she and her husband ran a corner grocery store. From this lengthy text, I selected portions that described the worsening situation in Russia and the actual travel . . . what made it to the final text was what I felt to be the "nugget" embedded in the larger story.

Each woman presents, among her larger writing, an important kernel which, when combined with the stories of the other women, forms a more complete picture of the whole.

Do you connect personally with these women's lives?

Yes. I really like these women. In every case, they are women I wish I had known personally. They were courageous, brave, and inspiring. I wish I had learned about them when growing up. It would have helped me in forming my own identity.

Another aspect of these women's lives that we learn about in the diaries is their feminism. In the early West, women were encouraged by their husbands to take on new roles. It was important that women step out from what had been previously understood as the feminine role model. In the West, a woman didn't just work in the family store, she often ran it.

Are there links between their stories and the ones from your family?

I suppose it's like the cobbler whose children don't have any shoes. I'm not as familiar as I should be with my own background. But there are links. The stories we remember are the ones that affect our lives the most.

For example, when I was a child, our family often spent Sundays picnicking in the Quebec countryside. My father, who loved to drive, was well known for his terrible sense of direction, and would invariably become lost while searching for our luncheon destination. Often the sandwiches had to be consumed in the car, since the picnic spot was impossible to locate. On many occasions, the "picnic" idea was abandoned altogether, and instead the family would opt for restaurant dining. We'd seek out the main street diner in towns like Saint Hyacinthe, Richelieu, and Cowansville. Thankful to finally get out of the car, we'd slump into the booths to hastily consume a very late lunch.

My father, on the other hand, would pop up from his seat and disappear for several minutes, reappearing with an animated expression on his face. "Guess what I've figured out?" he'd ask, and then quickly answer his own question. "There are four Cohens listed in this phone book! Can you believe that Jews live in this small town in the middle of nowhere?" My father's interest in how and why Jews lived in remote locations was the spark that ignited my same interest.

Another experience I remember occurred when I was about ten and visiting my grandparents' home in Manchester, England. My Grandma Ida had been a milliner as a young woman and she had a long history with the needle arts. My Grandpa Joe owned and operated textile mills in the City of Manchester, and designed many of the textiles he manufactured.

On this particular visit, my grandmother thought it was time for her Canadian grand-daughter to learn to sew. Many evenings were spent with her in front of the fire, practicing the art of needlepoint. After several nights sewing together, the back of my piece had become increasingly knotted and bulky due to the mistakes I'd made. I became frustrated and, with a single act of defiance, tossed it into the fire and stormed out of the room.

The next morning, my grandmother presented to me the very same piece of needle-point. She'd retrieved it from the fire, washed and ironed it, and now insisted I complete it. Needless to say, my grandmother won out. I did complete the needlepoint and her demands were a positive and lasting influence.

How do you go about gathering the information?

The gathering begins with archives all over the country. I've found stories at the American Jewish Archives in Cincinnati, the Western Jewish Center in Berkeley, various Jewish Historical Societies, and collections of women's manuscripts. Material relevant to Jewish women has long been subsumed within larger family collections, usually named for male relatives. . . . This is changing. There now exist several bibliographies and resource guides compiled exclusively for the purpose of researching women's history. The Jewish Women's Archive in Brookline, Massachusetts, is another excellent resource.

How do you balance the actual history with your own creative process?

My job as an artist is to develop a way of thinking about history and then to translate it visually. "Develop" is the pivotal word here. The story and the woman's voice are central to the artwork, upon which a broader theme can be advanced. It is of paramount impor-tance for me to maintain the integrity of each woman's story. If the text begins to serve as an appendage to the artwork, then, in my mind, I've failed. The quilting, stitching, and painting I employ remain secondary to the actual story. Maintaining this kind of integrity to the core history is perhaps part of why my work is taken seriously.

Can you describe the technical aspects of the process used in producing the digital prints on canvas?

The first step is to determine the story within the particular diary or memoir. Once the story has been selected, an actual quilt pattern is chosen from the standard and classic patterns that were popular during that era. For instance, Anna Marks's quilt is adapted from a pattern called "Duck-in-the-Mud," Sara Thal's quilt pattern is "Morning Star," and Fanny Sharlip's is "Cross and Crown." The quilt design is done digitally—I select the fabrics, then they are scanned into the computer and manipulated there. This portion of the process takes up to a month. The text and photo imagery is then added digitally.

The completed digital file is enlarged and printed on canvas at a commercial press and then returned to my studio in its large-format size, usually seven-by-seven feet. At this point, quilters from the community work with me to quilt cotton fabric sections over the printed imagery. On average, from start to finish, each quilt painting takes four to five months to complete.

How has this work affected your own religious identity?

The more I learn about how Jewish women have performed throughout history in the face of adversity my identification with Judaism grows stronger. I admire the ability to create order from chaos, to affirm that life is worth living even when it seems you are surrounded by darkness. These stories provide me with a direct connection to powerful human characteristics—courage, tolerance, hope, and pride. These women demonstrated these characteristics as part of their daily lives. Within the stories I share, I find a sister-hood, a community with which I am proud to identify.

CRAFTING MEMORY, PIECING HISTORY

Ten women speak from the centers of Andrea Kalinowski's quiltscapes. Fragments of memory, pieced together, sketch the patterns of an international diaspora, pushed to the North American West by poverty, persecution, and upheaval, drawn by hope and by families and friends who came before.

Immigrant women's domestic labor, religious practices, and community service forged a new cultural mosaic in the North American West, pieced from the diverse customs and faiths of global emigrations. Quilts aptly represent this complex cultural crossroads. Jewish women's neighbors might include Hopi, Lakota, Shoshone, and immigrants from Asia, Latin America, and Europe—as various as the fabrics and patterns women stitched into quilts for everyday use. Women's daily work transplanted cultures, built the West's farms and businesses, founded synagogues and churches, schools and libraries. They gleaned the time and resources to build communities much as they quilted, in fragments, and collectively with other women.

Women's daily labors were omitted from textbook histories, those national memories of battles, dates, and elections. Their words rarely survived to preserve a common legacy. Patchwork becomes a precise metaphor for the scraps of documents, letters, memoirs, and artifacts from which historians now piece together the larger patterns of the women's lives. The words patched on Kalinowski's quilt squares record common stories of wrenching leave-taking, difficult journeys, strange new surroundings, building homes, and adapting customs.

By 1880 some 250,000 Jews lived in the United States. Most emigrated from German-speaking countries between 1820–1880; many had come into contact with Reform Judaism and Neo-Orthodoxy. The few Jewish women inscribed in community histories were often the wives of an early merchant elite, women with the resources to support their public work as social reformers and organizers, who knit cross-cultural ties from a liberal understanding of Judaism and commitments to social reform and culture.

From 1880 through the 1920s, economic dislocations, rising birthrates, and anti-Semitism brought three million Jews from Russia, Romania, Hungary, and Galicia, most of whom practiced Orthodox Judaism. The promise of homestead land drew Jewish immigrants to the Canadian and U.S. Wests, sometimes with the help of organizations like the Jewish Agriculturalists' Aid Society of America and the Jewish Agricultural and Industrial Aid Society. Jewish agricultural communities and isolated Jewish homesteads dotted the western U.S. and Canada; individual homesteading was somewhat more common in the U.S., and Jewish agricultural colonies in Canada. In the U.S., single women could file for homesteads in their own names. Between 1882–1890, roughly 1,000 Jews filed for land in North and South Dakota alone, including many single Jewish women.

Jewish women lugged with them the resources to sustain Jewish life and identity: candlesticks, kiddush cups, challah covers, family photographs, and prayer books. They also carried the knowledge to prepare the Sabbath and Jewish holidays. They braided loaves of Sabbath challah, baked unleavened matzo for Passover, and the three-cornered hamentashen cookies for Purim. Each family recipe for gefilte fish, cholent, kreplach, chopped liver, kugel, latkes, matzo balls, or borscht carried a particular memory of survival from the Jewish communities of Russia, Poland, Germany, or Hungary— a heritage passed through generations of women.

The West brought unique challenges for observant Jewish women on isolated homesteads and ranches, or those who helped run family businesses in small towns. They must have a *mikvah* for ritual baths, keep kosher in communities where salt pork was a staple, maintain the Sabbath when their neighbors worked on Saturday. Some women relaxed their observance of kosher dietary laws; some Jewish men worked on Saturday or prayed without a *minyan*, the ten men required for services.

Gaining a foothold in the West was a gendered and generational process. It was harder for adult women to learn English than it was for their children and husbands, who used the language at school and in the marketplace. Men and children became bilingual and learned to negotiate a multicultural society; adult women spoke Yiddish and maintained Jewish homes. Often judged backward and unassimilated, married women sustained Jewish life, beginning with the children they bore, who traced their descent through their mothers. Much Jewish practice is home-centered. Those practices acquired even greater significance in the rural West where Jewish immigrants could rarely support synagogues. Over time, Jewish farmers joined an urban migration, using their hard-won land to finance further dreams in larger Jewish communities where children might attend religious schools and marry within the faith.

Women's domestic labor preserved ethnic and religious practices. Women who shared neither culture nor language forged multicultural communities, helping one another give birth, feed threshing crews, nurse the sick, and survive on scarce resources. Jewish women pieced new patterns of Jewish practice in the West, and with their neighbors forged an overlapping patchwork of western communities. Through Andrea Kalinowski's art, they speak from the centers of their lives to craft a collective legacy.

ELIZABETH JAMESON

Imperial Oil & Lincoln McKay Chair of American Studies
Department of History, University of Calgary

FOR FURTHER READING

Judith Reesa Baskin, *Jewish Women in Historical Perspective* (Detroit: Wayne State University Press, 1991).

Susannah Heschel, *Women in Judaism* (New York: Schocken Books, 1983).

The Jewish Historical Society of Southern Alberta, *Land of Promise: The Jewish Experience in Southern Alberta* (Calgary: JHSSA, 1996).

Kenneth Libo and Irving Howe, *We Lived There, Too: In Their Own Words and Pictures—Pioneer Jews and the Westward Movement of America, 1630–1930* (New York: St. Martin's/Marek, 1984).

H. Elaine Lindgren, *Land in Her Own Name: Women Homesteaders in North Dakota* (Norman: University of Oklahoma Press, 2nd ed. 1996).

Natalie Ornish, *Pioneer Jewish Texans* (Dallas: Texas Heritage Press, 1989).

Sheryll Patterson-Black, "Women Homesteaders on the Great Plains Frontier," *Frontiers* 1:2 (Spring 1976): 67–88.

Harriet Rochlin and Fred Rochlin, *Pioneer Jews: New Life in the Far West* (Boston: Houghton Mifflin, 1984).

Claudia Rodin, *The Book of Jewish Food* (New York: Viking, 1997).

Linda Mack Schloff, *"And Prairie Dogs Weren't Kosher": Jewish Women in the Upper Midwest Since 1855* (St. Paul: Minnesota Historical Society Press, 1996).

Ellen Umansky and Dianne Ashton, *Four Centuries of Jewish Women's Spirituality: A Sourcebook* (Boston: Beacon Press, 1992).

Ruthe Weingarten and Cathy Schechter, *Deep in the Heart: The Lives and Legends of Texas Jews* (Austin: Eakin Press, 1990).